Query Based Text Summarizat ....ny
Approach

Zarah Zainab
Muzamil Shah

Query Based Text Summarization using Machine learning Approach

Learning Approaches

LAP LAMBERT Academic Publishing

Publisher:
LAP LAMBERT Academic Publishing
is a trademark of
International Book Market Service Ltd., member of OmniScriptum Publishing Group
17 Meldrum Street, Beau Bassin 71504, Mauritius

Printed at: see last page
ISBN: 978-613-9-45282-8

Dedication

This thesis is dedicated to our parents, teachers, friends especially our supervisor Mr. Qazi Haseeb Yousaf for their endless support and encouragement. Their guidelines made our way smooth and easier. We will always appreciate whatever they have done to support us throughout our academic session.

Acknowledgments

As a matter of first importance, we are truly grateful to Allah the most generous and most merciful. We might want to express our deep-felt appreciation to our supervisor Mr. Qazi Haseeb Yousaf for being so kind to support and for being available throughout the project while sharing his knowledge and guiding us. We are especially thankful to our friends and fellows from the core of our hearts as they were being so supportive and helpful to through all time.

Muzamil Shah

Zarah Zainab

February, 2019

Abstract

Extraction of relevant information on a specific query from rapidly growing data is a concern for quiet time in order to scan and analyze data from all the related documents. Therefore, text summarization is paramount research area these days. It is about to find most relevant information from single or multi-documents. A reasonable amount of work is done in this area to overcome extensive searching and to reduce the time required. The knowledge-based and machine learning are the two methods for query-based text summarization where Machine learning approaches are mostly used for calculating probabilistic feature using Natural Language Processing (NLP) tools and techniques for both supervised and unsupervised learning. In the first part of this research work include to identify and analyze machine learning approaches for query-based text summarization for finding a useful summary for the users as specified by their need. In the second part, a comprehensive discussion is done to present the internal working mechanism of machine learning approaches for query-based text summarization. In the third part, this work the analysis of 32 linear combinations of most used features are analyzed in order to get the best feature combination. In the fourth part, the comparative analysis on Query Likelihood Model and the Vector Space Model being analyzed. The result of the Query Likelihood Model is more accurate than the Vector Space Model. Finally, this shows the limitation of the Vector Space Model over Query Likelihood Model.

Table of Contents

List of Figure

List of Tables

Chapter 1

Introduction

Natural Language Processing (NLP) is a field of computer science that provides interaction between the computer and human language. Supervised and unsupervised machine learning techniques are used to solve NLP problems these days. The increase in digital data and information (Asthana et al. 2017). It is difficult to retrieve the related information according to the user demand. The data scientists worked in the area of machine learning approaches to automate the information retrieval process. Automatic text document summarization is an interdisciplinary research area of computer science that includes Artificial Intelligence (AI), Data Mining, Statistics as well as Psychology. It has a variety of applications like summaries of newspapers, articles, books, magazines, scientific paper, weather forecasting, stock marketing and news headlines (Das and F. T. Martins 2016). Text Summarization depends upon the understanding of languages according to the context. Language is different for different genres have different writing styles, semantic meaning and sentence structure i.e. Research papers, blogs, twitter, single or multiple documents, emails, and search engines. A strong framework is required for considering the data in a human way which is a key factor to define a summarizer's task in automated text summarization. In single or multi-documents, the purpose of summarizer can be either generic, query-based or domain specific.

1.1 Background Study

Text Summarization is the process of extracting central information from the original text document. The extracted information is generated as a condensed report which acts as a concise summary to the user. It is very difficult for humans to understand and interpret the content of the text (Das and F. T. Martins 2016). The use of automatic tools for information processing became essential to the user. It is very difficult to exploit all the relevant information available online without using those tools. Automatic text summarization systems are very useful. It allows the user to obtain the relevant information. In recent years, Natural Language Processing (NLP) and Information Retrieval (IR) communities have shown a great interest in automatic text summarization (Jaoua and Hamadou 2008). Text Summarization comes under the umbrella of NLP because text summarization depends upon an understanding the language. To apply machine learning techniques to Natural Language Processing (NLP), it usually needs to convert the unstructured data to structured data. It is more efficient rather than predefined rules for information retrieval. Machine learning techniques have many benefits i.e; first, it provides an easy means of incorporating a wide range of features. Second, depending on the machine learning technique, the model can be learned over a rich function space (Metzler and Kanungo 2008). Text document summarization playing an important role in Information Retrieval (IR) because, it condenses a large pool of information into a concise form, through selecting the relevant sentences and discards redundant sentences and termed it as summarization process (Yadav and Sharan 2015).Text summarization is categorized in the following classes. These are as follow (Zhai et al. 2008): -

1.1.1 Abstractive summarization

In Abstractive text summarization, the main concept of a document is focused.It produces the summarized information in a coherent form that is easily readable and grammatically correct by making modification in the original text (Das and F. T. Martins 2016).

1.1.2 Extractive summarization

In Extractive approaches, the related sentences are extracted and are ranked by their importance. Then the sentences are grouped together to compose the summary without making changes and modification in an original text document (Rahman and Borah 2015).

1.1.3 Query-based summary

Query-based text summarization is very important as it gives information as required by the user. The user does a not need to spend a long time searching or browsing for the required information. The rapid increase in online information, the query-based summarization plays a vital role in the information retrieval process. To find the relevant

2

information according to the user's query (Rahman and Borah 2015). The query-based summarization is sometimes also called "user-focused summarization. In Query focus Text summarization, the importance of each sentence will be determined by the combination of two factors. These are (Hasselqvist, Helmertz, and Kågebäck 2017): -

i. How Relevant is the sentence to the user Question?

ii. How important is the sentence in the context of the input in which it appears?

1.2 Problem statement

Identification and analysis of machine learning approach for Query-based text summarization for a single a document.

1.3 Research Questions of the study

RQ1: Which approaches to machine learning available for query-based text summarization?

RQ2: What is the mechanism of discussed approaches?

RQ3: What are the applicable areas of discussed approaches?

RQ4: What are the limitations of ML approaches in query-based text summarization?

1.4 Scope and Objectives

1.4.1 Scope

Text summarizations give a scope of study both in Information Retrieval systems and Text Mining system. Automated summarization is an important area in NLP research. It consists of automatically creating a summary of one or more texts. When it comes to applying a technique, defining a summarizer's task is a key factor. For example, the summarizer will work on either single document or multi-document and the purpose of summarizer can be either generic or query-based summarization.

1.4.2 Objectives

i. To study a possible set of machine learning approaches for query-based text summarization.

3

ii. To represent the mechanism of the possible algorithms using query-based text summarization.

iii. To explore the different areas where these algorithms are applicable.

iv. To find limitations of such algorithms.

Chapter 2
Literature Review

A large amount of data these days are available on different resources such as the World Wide Web, news articles, books, and emails. The shortage of time user wants to excess data and information according to their need. The automatic text summarization is one of the techniques that enable the user to access the most important information timely. the query oriented summarization techniques by extracting the most informative sentences (Afsharizadeh 2018) discussed. The number of features is extracted from the sentences and scores are assigned based on its feature values. Then the high ranked sentences are selected to be present in the summary. Language Modeling is an important part of Text summarization (Zhai and Lafferty 2001).Query likelihood works on Maximum likelihood between the query and the document. Maximum Likelihood is extremely important for information retrieval from a single document. The explosion of the Internet encourages the development of techniques for organizing and presenting information to users in an effective way. Query-focused multi-document summarization (MDS) methods have been proposed as one such technique that gains the attention in recent years. The query-focused MDS (Zhai et al. 2008) is used to synthesize a brief (often fixed-length) and well-organized summary from a set of topic-related documents to answer a complex question or address a topic statement. The author (L. Wang, Raghavan, Castelli, et al. 2016) discussed the different role of sentence compression techniques for query-focused MDS.Three types of approaches to sentence-compression is discussed i.e. rule-based, sequence-based and tree-based. Query-focused MDS framework consisting of three steps: Sentence Ranking, Sentence Compression, and Post-processing. A generic summary (Das and F. T. Martins 2016) provides a general sense of the document's contents. In generic summarization when a specific query is an input, then it is difficult to extract the central topic from the document set. To interpret the narrative in ways that will concur with the design of a purely BE-based summarizer. (Zhou, Lin, and Hovy 2005) presents the model for query-based multi-document summarization based on Basic Element (BE) for generic summarizations gives high-informative unigrams, bigrams and longer units of a text, which can be built up compositionally interpret topic-based queries which count units for frequency-based topic identification. The rapid increase in online information, the query-based summarization plays a vital role in the information retrieval process. (Varadarajan and Hristidis 2006) presented a structure-based technique to create query-specific summaries for text documents. In this model first to create the document graph of a document to represent the hidden semantic structure of the document. Then perform keyword proximity search on this graph. The text is an entity, where words, sentences, phrases, and paragraphs are connected to each other in a semantic way known as semantic relation. Natural text can be represented as language network. Language network is formed by considering the words or concepts as nodes. The relation between them is represented as edges of the network. Once a text is represented as a network a variety of techniques can be implemented over it for different analysis from a different perspective.(Das and F. T. Martins 2016) the proposed semantic graph for summarization of text document. The semantic graph is independent of any language. This proposed approach gives importance to semantic importance of the word present in the document which can be applied to a small document where TF-IDF cannot be used. Data and information increasing day by day and moving ahead toward big data. The need for automatic text summarization is required that can summarized text (Das and F. T. Martins 2016). The information in the compressed and summarized form having semantic meaning is needed. The problems with multi-document summarization i.e redundancy, identifying difference among documents and summary coherence. The main focus is on Abstractive Text Summarization. The objective of abstractive summarization is to produce a generalized summary. It conveys information in a precise way that generally requires advance language generation and compression techniques. The key challenges mentioned by the author is still a research area for researchers i.e.; there is no generalized framework for parsing and alignment.Extraction of the important sentences and sentence ordering according to the original text different techniques are proposed by different researchers i.e one of the technique is Support Vector Machine (SVM). Author (Zhao et al. 2008) applied regression model for query focused multi-document. The support vector regression (SVR) is used to calculate the importance of a sentence in a document. It summarized through a set of pre-defined features in the paper. The learning model used is based on a fixed set of feature-based approach to search for an optimum composite scoring function. Sentences are scored according to their feature values. Features play an important role in sentence scoring and ranking. The experiments have shown that regression models are preferred over classification models or learning-to-rank models for estimating the importance of the sentences. The use of regression-based machine learning techniques, such as support vector regression (SVR) and gradient boosted decision trees (GBDTs), is used for the sentence selection task, which is an important sub-task of constructing query-based abstracts and summaries(Metzler and Kanungo 2008). (Teng et al. 2008) the proposed approach for single document summaries based on local topic identification and word frequency is proposed. The logical Structure feature which has been successfully applied for multi-document summarization. Documents are cluster into the local topic after sentences similarity is calculated which are sorted later based on the score. Sentences from all local topics are selected by computing the word frequency. The proposed method improves the information redundancy of each local topic is reduced. The local topic identification author proposed the vector space model. It picks the best sentence from the best local topic if the desired summary length has not been reached. The sum is obtained using the probabilistic model of document weight and Topic weight. Sentence location plays an important role in the summarization. The author also determines it and then make a summary. The new approach for single document summaries based on local topic identification and word frequency. Query-based text summarization is very important as it gives information as required by the user. The user does not need to spend a long time searching or browsing for the required information. The author (El-Haj and Hammo 2008) performed query based text summarization on the Arabic language. The system produces a query-oriented summary for a single Arabic document. The use of traditional vector space model and cosine similarity to extract the relevant passage and produce its summary. The lack of public-domain tools for Arabic as

7

compare to the English Language. The redundancy problem is one of the major problems in text summarization that cannot be totally resolved and still have research area to be explored the author (Jaoua and Hamadou 2008) descript a model or detailed of determining the criteria that can be used to extract sentences from multiple documents. The proposed method by the author in the paper uses a genetic algorithm to generate a population of extracts. Then it evaluates them and classifies them in order to produce the best extract. The genetic algorithm starts from a random solution, and then it builds, in each stage, a set of solutions and evaluates them. The genetic algorithm produces, for each iteration, an extract's population while combining, randomly, sentences from the various documents. Then apply crossover and mutation operators. It assigns, for each generated extract, an objective value, which depends on criteria applied to extract as a whole unit. The importance of statistical criteria to determine the candidate sentences to form the extract i.e. Position of the sentence, Size of the document, TF*IDF, Similarity to the title, Similarity to document keywords, Similarity to question keywords.

A query expansion algorithm used in the graph-based ranking approach for query-focused multi-document summarization (Zhao, Wu, and Huang 2009). It resolves the problem of information limit in the original query. The approach works on both the sentence-to-sentence relations and the sentence-to-word relations to select the query based informative words from the document set and use them as query expansions to improve the sentence ranking result. (Wan 2010) introduced the novel unified approach simultaneously for a single document and as well as multi-document summarization by making the use of mutual influences between the two tasks. In this model, the mutual influence between two tasks is incorporated into a graph model. The ranking scores of a sentence for two tasks can be obtained in the unified ranking process. The models are known as Unified graph-based framework. Feature selection is also an essential part of Information Retrieval (Profile, Summarization, and Extraction 2010) proposed a clustering method for multi-document classification and summarization. In this approach, the cluster of multi-documents is labeled or grouped according to the user requirement. The related documents are grouped in their cluster. Then feature profiling is generated on the cluster by considering the features i.e; word weight, sentence position, sentence length, sentence centrality, proper nouns in the sentences and numerical data in the sentence. Then the scores of features are calculated against each individual sentence. The selected sentences are arranged in the chronological order according to the position of the sentence in the original document. The summary generated using the proposed method also compared with the human-generated summary for evaluation.(Judith D. Schlesinger, Deborah J.Baker 2011) proposed a model for extracting the sentences for the summary by calculating a score for each sentence using features including the document title, the location of a sentence in the document, clustering of significant words and the occurrence of user-supplied query terms. The feature considered by an author in the paper are; Number of unique query terms in a sentence, number of tokens in a sentence, a distance of sentence from one with a query term, the position of a sentence in a document, paragraph position. The set of the feature is applied to simple linear regression. Text Summarization is the challenging task to retrieve the required data or information from the bulk of data(Siva Kumar, Premchand, and Govardhan 2011). Summarization allows the user to understand the full document by reading the summary. Data compression or reduction plays important role in information retrieval according to the request of the user in the form of query. The author of the paper performed query-based test summarization based on similarity of the sentence and word frequency using a vector space model. The vector space model will be used to find a similar sentence in the document against the user query and the sum focus on the total word frequency. The proposed method in this paper worked by grouping the similar sentences and word frequency and removes the redundancy which is still a problem for text summarization.(Shen and Li 2011) introduced a supervised learning method to sentence extraction in multi-document summarization. The sentence labels for training corpus from the existing human labeling data in form of <query, document set, and human summaries>.In the proposed method for text summarization based on ranking. The use of ranking SVM learning to rank method, to train the feature weights for query-focused multi-document summarization. To construct the training data for ranking SVM, a rank label of "summary sentence" or "non-summary sentence" needs to be assigned to the training sentences. Information Retrieving is a field in which a high level of progress is taking place. It is playing an important role in searching on the internet and in query-based processing. (Jain, Bewoor, and Patil 2012) introduced Open NLP tool for Natural Language Processing of text for word matching. And to extract meaningful and query dependent information from a large set of offline documents, data mining document clustering algorithm is adopted. Text classification is used to assign labels to unassigned document into predefined categories. The documents can be converted into such format that documents can be recognized by a classifier. (Ko 2012) proposed the Vector space model. In this model, the documents are represented in the form of vectors. The use of Tf-Idf weightage is to convert the document in such format that improves text classification. The term weighting is utilized for text classification by the author. The proposed methodology of the paper performed consistently well on two benchmark data sets and KNN and SVM classifier. The query-focused summary has to provide brief, well-organized information in a short paragraph (two or three sentences). According to (Damova and Kliment 2014) the pyramid method addresses the problem by using multiple human summaries to create a gold-standard and by exploiting the frequency of information in the human summaries in order to assign importance to different facts. The pyramids annotations are a valuable source of information for training automatically text summarization systems using Machine Learning techniques. The author explores different possibilities for applying them in training SVMs to rank sentences in order of relevance to the query. Structural, cohesion-based and query-dependent features are used for training. (Gupta and Siddiqui 2012) worked on query focused multi-document summarization by combining single document summary using sentence clustering. The syntactic and semantic similarity between sentences is used for clustering. Single document summary is generated using document feature, sentence reference index feature, location feature, and concept similarity feature. Sentences from single document summaries are clustered and topmost sentences from each cluster are used for creating a multi-document summary. The document and queries are presented in different languages must be translated into some specific language.

Cross-lingual information retrieval (CLIR) is a special case of Information Retrieval in which queries and documents are presented in different languages. In CLIR the language barrier is removed by converting the language of the query into the language of the document. (Ture and Boschee 2014) introduce the novel method for learning optimal combination weights to build a linear combination of existing query translation approaches. (Durrett et al. 2014) present the discriminative model of summarization of the single document. It combines compression and Anaphoricity constraints. Anaphoricity constraints improve the cross-sentence coherence. It rewrites the pronouns to make them explicitly mention. These pronoun rewrites are scored in the objective and introduced into the length constraint to make sure they do not cause the summary to be too long. The compression model is integrated to enforce grammatically as well as Anaphoricity constraints to enforce coherence. There is a different application of Query-Based Summarization i.e; retrieval of headlines from e-Newspaper, question answering, summarization, extracting salient features and searching. (Sankarasubramaniam, Ramanathan, and Ghosh 2014) a used novel approaches to leverage Wikipedia in conjunction with graph-based ranking. In this approach, the first step is to construct a bipartite sentence and then rank the input sentence using iterative updates on that graph. Then, it takes up personalized and query-focused summarization, where the sentence ranks additionally depend on user interests and queries, respectively. Finally, the author presents a Wikipedia-based multi-document summarization algorithm.An important feature of the proposed algorithms to enable real-time incremental summarization. The users can first view an initial summary, and then request additional content if interested. Automatic text summarization is the task of producing a concise and fluent summary while preserving key information content and overall meaning there are three methods on the of which one sentence is considered to be the part of text summary i.e cue method, title method, and location method. The focus of the author is extractive summarization method and provides an overview of some for the most dominant approaches in this category. (Damova and Kliment 2014) review the different processes for summarization and try to describe the effectiveness and shortcoming (problem or failure) faced by different methods (Yousefi Azar et al. 2015) of the paper proposed the ENAE Model using inputs with added noise and apply a deep neural network to obtain query based extractive summarization. The model is in the paper using the deep autoencoder to test their model on emails by considering the" the subject of the email" as a query. It presents the short summaries of the relevant email. It was tested on both single and multi-threads of mail considering it as a single document. Extractive approaches which rank sentences by importance. Summarization is the process of reducing a text document in such a way that retains the important points of the original document. The extractive summarizers work to extract the sentences that convey the best message hidden in the text. Manual extraction or annotation of keywords is a tedious process involving lots of manual efforts and time. (Thomas, Bharti, and Babu 2016) proposed such algorithm in the paper that compares the articles having a similar title in four different e-Newspapers. It checks the similarity and consistency in summarized results. In the paper different Machine learning approaches because Keyword extraction is a learning problem. The HMM model a supervised learning model for keyword extraction is used. (Rahman and Borah 2015) also focuses on the query-based text summarization using Extractive summarization techniques. The efforts had been made to go through various extractive based approaches for the query to find the relative summary for the user as their need. The unsupervised learning model i.e. Document Graph approach and Feature-based model being discussed. Summarization is one of the techniques to represent the information in a concise way with equal sense. Text document summarization is a part of Information Retrieval (IR). (Yadav and Sharan 2015) proposed a hybrid method for single text document summarization. It is a linear combination of statistical features i.e sentence position, centroid, TF-IDF and semantic features. Most of the query-based text summarization explores methods that generate summaries-based queries regardless of user preferences.(Valizadeh and Brazdil 2015) present the study how to use machine learning to identify how user summarized their text. The model proposed in the paper finds a relationship between the sentences by detecting actor-object relationship (AOR). In this model, the importance is given to those sentences which satisfy the actor-object relationship. Text summarization is one of the problems under Natural Language Processing.(Km, Vishwa, and Km 2016) represents two techniques i.e Clustering and Support Vector Machine (SVM) used to solve NLP problems. The hybrid approach is used by cascading both techniques for improving the summary. It helps in summarizing the text documents with more efficiency by avoiding the redundancy among the document with the highest relevance to the input query. The proposed system provides a summary of both single and multiplies related documents. The category extraction algorithm (L. Wang, Raghavan, Cardie, et al. 2016) builds a category that stores the categories and semantic links between categories from a certain domain. In the defined approach the user inputs a question; keywords are extracted from it by using Natural Language Processing Toolkit. The distance is then calculated between the categories. The top N sentences closest to the question. The shortest distance of top N answers is selected. The Dijkstra algorithm is used for calculating the distance. (X. Wang, Xu, and Zhuge 2016) used category space extraction from Wikipedia to find answers from a single document. (Litvak 2017) discussed the unsupervised method for query-based extractive summarization based on Minimum Description Length (MDL) that applies Krimp compression Algorithm. The main idea behind is to select frequent word sets related to a given query that would compress into summary information. MDL principle is defining the best summary. It could lead to the best compression of the text with query-related information. In future, the authors of the paper improve their work by trying Word Vectors Method. This method assumed to be better in order to have a better matching word in question and sentences. Ranking a sentence according to the user query is of the key step in Information Retrieval. (L. Wang, Raghavan, Cardie, et al. 2016) that there is a central topic (or query) on which a user is seeking diverse opinions. It predicts query-relevance through automatically learned statistical rankers. The ranking function not only aims to find sentences that are on the topic of the query but also ones that are "opinionated" through the use of several features that indicate subjectivity and sentiment. The relevance score is encoded in a submodular function. Diversity is accounted for by a dispersion function that maximizes the pairwise distance between the pairs of sentences

13

selected. According to the author, the framework used in the paper is capable of including statistically learned sentence relevance and encouraging the summary to cover diverse topics. Summaries generated from text documents with respect to queries known as query-based summarization. (Hasselqvist, Helmertz, and Kågebäck 2017) introduced Neural Networks for query-based text summarization. (Jo 2017) propose the KNN algorithm. The similarity between the feature vectors was computed by considering the similarity feature and their values. The use of text summarizer is to identify the importance and unimportance of sentence or paragraph using binary classification. In the paper, the similarity is considered on the basis of both attribute and its values. The goal is to implement the text summarization algorithm which takes represent data item more compactly and provide more reliability.

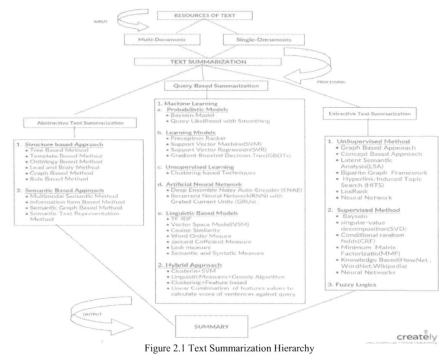

Figure 2.1 Text Summarization Hierarchy

2.1 Machine Learning Approaches

Text summarization has different types that can be achieved by applying different techniques. Machine learning approaches now days are also being used to convert a large pool of data into a concise summary. The focus of this research is to take a survey of Query based text summarization and identify the Machine learning approaches for Query-based Text summarization as discussed

2.1.1 Probabilistic Models:

a. Query Likelihood with Smoothing

Query likelihood works on Maximum likelihood between the query and the document. The term smoothing refers to the adjustment of maximum likelihood estimator of a language model to achieve accuracy. It is used not to assign a zero probability to unseen words. Maximum Likelihood is extremely important for information retrieval from a single document.

In the first part weight of each term common between the query and document is calculated (i.e., matched terms). In the second part only, a document-dependent constant that is related to how much probability mass will be allocated to unseen words, according to the particular smoothing method used. The Jelinek-Mercer method generally performs well but it works better for long queries than for title queries. The Dirichlet prior method also performs well but it works better for concise title queries than for long queries. It is really important to understand the smoothing on(Metzler and Kanungo 2008)(Zhai and Lafferty 2001).

2.1.2 Learning models

a. Support Vector Machines (SVM) using pyramid annotations

In the paper Support Vector Machines (SVM) is used to detect relevant information form a query-focused summary. Several SVMs are trained using information from pyramids. The Pyramid method addresses the problem by using human summaries to create a gold-standard of relevant sentences extracted from the human summaries document. The

Importance to the summaries are assigned in the order it has same tokens frequency in the human summaries the sentences that are part of the summary if have a match with original documents have an impact in a positive and negative sense. Then the given query and a set of Documents, the trained SVMs are used to rank sentences. The top-ranked ones are checked to avoid Redundancy using a percentage overlapping measure. The pyramid annotations are a valuable source of. Information for training automatically texts summarization systems using Machine Learning techniques. The feature set must be explored more to identify such feature of query and document that can lead to more accuracy. In training SVMs to rank sentences in order of relevance to the query. Structural, cohesion-based. And query-dependent features are used for training (Fuentes, Alfonseca, and Rodr 2007).

b. Support Vector Regression (SVR) and Gradient Boosted Decision Trees (GBDTs)

Document summaries can be of two types. These include query independent summary

And query dependent summary. The given query and a document, a query dependent abstract is generated as follows. The relevant (with respect to the query) Sentences or passages within the document must be identified. This is referred to as the sentence selection problem. After the relevant sentences have been identified, the composition Phase begins. When composing an abstract, it is important to consider how many sentences to include, and how to compress the sentences to fit within a fixed bounding box. The machine learning techniques used to solve the sentence selection problem. There are several benefits to using such techniques. First, they provide an easy means of incorporating a wide range of features. Second, depending on the machine learning technique used, the model can be learned over a rich function space. The features are divided into two categories i.e.

Query-dependent feature: theses feature an attempt to capture how relevant a given sentence S is to the query Q. These include an exact match, Overlap, Overlap-synonyms

Query-Independent feature: The goal of query independent features is to encode any prior knowledge we have about individual sentences. i.e., sentence length, sentence

16

location. Identification of proper feature set feature sets available as the mark so that other researchers can develop and evaluate. Learning to rank techniques for the sentence selection task which has very different characteristics than the typical ad-hoc and web retrieval tasks (Metzler and Kanungo 2008).

c. SVR as Regression Models

SVR is used as a regression model. Support vector regression (SVR) is used to calculate the importance of a sentence in a document. It summarized through a set of pre-defined features in the paper. The learning model used in the paper is based on a fixed set of feature-based approach to search for an optimum composite scoring function. Sentences are scored according to their feature values; the features play an important role in sentence scoring and rankings which largely depends on the choice of kernels. There is no theory concerning how to choose a good kernel function in a data-dependent way (Ouyang et al. 2010).

d. Perceptron ranker as supervised learning algorithm and skewed word Distribution

The perceptron ranker is used for ranking sentences. The algorithm learns a parameter vector of weights, as well as a vector of rank boundaries. The weight vector is combined with a given feature vector via an inner-product to calculate the score of the sample. In skewed word Distribution, it skews the word distributions towards the query in a document set by adding the counts of each of the non-stop query words, multiplied by an empirically determined factor, to the counts of words in the document set. When extracting features from a sentence, words that are in the query will have relatively larger feature values, by virtue of having higher document set counts. The sentences are first ranked using the skewing approach described above, and the output from this step (the SoftMax normalized perceptron score) is one of the features inputs to the ranker.

This work present query directed summarization in three tasks:

Text normalization and segmentation: which include preprocessing of text where the text is normalized where unnecessary things are removed excluding stemming and stemming

Sentence ranking: this includes two types of ranking for retrieving the document or sentence in the document. One is Query neutral ranking and other Query focused ranking. **Sentence Selection**: Sentence is selected from the rank list have some restriction on the bases of which sentence is selected from the ranking list to be part of the summary.

It is based on using a supervised algorithm for this reason two separate models are trained. One with a large collection of documents clusters trained over query neutral manual summaries. Other with a small collection of documents trained over query focused which includes clusters and association with manual summaries. The limitation of the approach is that it does not perform any query expansion. Query expansion should work well with the word distribution approach, and it appears to help other systems significantly (Fisher and Roark 2006)

2.1.3 Unsupervised Learning

a. The clustering-based approach

Sentence-clustering algorithm is fully unsupervised, and it does not assume any prior knowledge. Cluster-ordering algorithm orders clusters based on the cluster importance, which is computed by the sum of the weights of the content words of a cluster. The importance of a cluster based on the number of important words it contains. The importance of a sentence is based on local. Importance and global importance of the words contained in it. The local importance of a word in a cluster indicates how much the word contributes in the formation of the central concept and the global Importance indicates how the word contributes in the formation of multiple different concepts (sub-topics) spread over the input collection of documents (Sarkar 2009).

b. Sentence Clustering

Query focused multi-document summarization is combined with single document summary using sentence clustering. Following are steps to perform the cluster on sentence. The syntactic and semantic Similarity between sentences is used for clustering. Single document summary is generated using the following features i.e. document feature, sentence reference index feature, location feature, and concept Similarity feature.

Sentences from single document summaries are clustered. The top-most sentences from each cluster are used for creating a multi-document summary. Sentences from each cluster are extracted to create multi-document summarization. The extracted sentences are arranged according to their position in the original document (Gupta and Siddiqui 2012).

2.1.4 Linguistic Models:

a. Vector Space Model

In the vector space model, the documents and the query are represented as vectors. Each vector has one component for every distinct term that appears in the entire document collection. To reflect the relative importance of each term in a document.

System Description:

The system gives summarized document in main two modules

Document Selection: this process includes the tokenization of query to extract the query token which includes removal of stop word. Query token is used to retrieve the documents that are more related to the query

Document Summarizer: All documents that are already retrieved against query are marge into paragraphs using tokenization. It is including more the one document and become a single document having multiple paragraphs. After this, the relevant paragraph is extracted by calculating the similarity between the document and the query using the Vector Space Model Equation as shown in equation 4.1 (El-Haj and Hammo 2008).

$$W_{ij} = \frac{TF_{ij} \times IDF_j}{\sqrt{\sum_{j=1}^{i} (w_{ij})^2}}$$

Eq 2.1

b. Sentence Similarity Measures

Similarity measures are also the part of Machine Learning, Data Mining, and text processing text depends upon the usage and scenario. The techniques are: -Word

Overlapping Measures are: Jaccard Similarity Coefficient, Simple Word Overlap, and IDF Overlap Measures, Phrasal Overlap Measure-IDF Measures-IDF Vector Similarity, Word Order Similarity, Semantic and Syntactic Measures

The similarity between natural language sentences is critical to the performance of several applications such as text mining, question answering, and text summarization. In information retrieval, the similarity measure is used to assign a ranking score between a query and texts in a corpus. Question answering application requires similarity identification (Achananuparp et al. 2008).

Word Overlapping Measures: - similarity score based on a number of words shared by two sentences. In this work, we consider four words overlap measures: Jaccard similarity coefficient, simple word overlaps, IDF overlap, and phrasal overlap.

Jaccard similarity coefficient is a similarity measure that compares the similarity between two feature sets. The overlap measures compute the similarity between sentence pairs.

i. IDF overlap is the proportion of words that appear in both sentences weighted by their inverse document frequency.

ii. Phrasal Overlap Measure is a relationship between the length of phrases and their frequencies in a text collection.

iii. TF-IDF Vector similarity the standard TF-IDF similarity is defined as cosine similarity between vector representations of two sentences.

iv. Word Order Similarity checks the order between the documents

v. Semantic and Syntactic Measures in which the semantic meaning as well as a syntactic measure also important.

Linguistics measures perform relatively poor in judging dissimilar pairs in high-complexity data sets. The word overlap and TF-IDF measures tend to reject many dissimilar sentence pairs since their proportion of overlap or the word occurrence is smaller in high-complexity datasets due to the difference in sentence pair lengths(Achananuparp, Hu, and Shen 2008).

20

2.1.5 Artificial Neural Network

a. Graph-based approach

A query expansion algorithm used in the graph-based ranking approach for query-focused multi-document summarization. The approach makes the use of both sentence-to-sentence relationships and sentence-to-word Relationships to select expansion words from the documents. This Method the expansion words satisfy both information richness and query relevance. The algorithmic steps i.e. Use a graph-based ranking algorithm to rank all the sentences in the documents where the original query is used. Perform our query expansion method based on the ranking results in step 1 and update the query. Use the newly expanded query to perform a graph-based ranking algorithm again for sentence ranking. Impose a redundancy penalty on the ranked sentences to obtain their final overall scores, which are used for summary generation(Zhao, Wu, and Huang 2009).

b. Deep Neural Network

Deep neural networks have gained popularity in a wide variety of applications, in particular, they have been successfully applied to various natural language processing (NLP) tasks.

Deep Ensemble Noisy Auto-Encoder (ENAE) that combines the top-ranked sentences from multiple runs on the same input with different added noise for query-based extractive summarization. The steps how the algorithm works: i.e. Train the AE on all sentences and queries in the corpus. Use the trained AE to get the latent representations for each query and each sentence in the document; Rank the sentences using their latent representations to choose the query-related sentences to be included in the summary.

Once the AE model has been trained, it can be used to extract the latent representations for each sentence in each document and for each query. We assume that the AE will place the sentences with a similar semantic meaning close to each other in the latent space and thus, we can use those representations to rank the sentences according to their relevance to the query (Yousefi Azar et al. 2015).

c. Recurrent Neural Networks (RNN)

A Recurrent Neural Network **(RNN)** is a class of artificial neural network where connections between nodes form a directed graph along a sequence. **RNNs** can use their internal state (memory) to process sequences of inputs.

Grated Current Units (GRUs) give you much better representations of sequences and are generally able to perform more complex transformations with high reliability. They were successfully used in neural machine translation in the last years.

These both above models are the sequential model they deal with sequential data. The Algorithm mechanism steps are as follows:

i. Input a document and a query these are sequences of words.

ii. Then it passes a document to document encoder and query to a query encoder respectively.

iii. The encoder's outputs are then passed to the attentive decoder, which generates a summary. Both encoders, as well as the decoder, use RNNs with GRUs.

2.1.6 Hybrid Approaches

a. Hybrid Approach i.e.; Clustering and SVM

This approach targeting the multiple related documents text summarization using the cluster. The previous work uses the Support Vector Machine to Solve Natural language Processing (NLP) problem. In this work, they have proposed a hybrid approach of Cluster and SVM which gives more efficiency by avoiding the redundancy among the document and ensure the highest relevance against the input query.

Preprocessing included Tokenization, Removal of Stop words, convert to lower case, Stemming and Lemmatization.

Clustering included vector space model for finding the n-dimensional and for similarity measure between the query and document(Km, Vishwa, and Km 2016).

b. Minimum description length (MDL) principle and Association Rules.

The work is based on query-focused text summarization using minimum description length that applies the compression to the selected sentence which is scored at the top. In this proposed work Sentences in all documents are considered as Transaction where using frequent itemset is found by using Apriori and TID algorithms. This algorithm is used because processing of large dataset needs a huge amount of time and this technique will avoid more than half of dataset because of the nature of these algorithms where query related text does not exist. Summary construction is based on Coding table which has minimized encoded sentence ranking for summary construction explain in paper with detail. Our preprocessing for query and documents includes

i.   Sentence splitting
ii. Tokenization
iii. Stop word removal
iv. Too long or too short are omitted
v.   The query is considered to be the set of stemmed tokens (Litvak 2017)

c. Linguistic Measure approach and the Greedy Algorithm

A query-based summarization method, which uses a combination of semantic relations between words and their syntactic composition, to extract meaningful sentences from document sets is introduced.

The method is executed by computing the semantic and syntactic similarity of the sentence-to-sentence and sentence- to-query. To reduce redundancy in summary, this method uses the greedy algorithm to impose diversity penalty on the sentences. In addition, the proposed method expands the words in both the query and the sentences to tackle the problem of information limit. The Algorithmic steps are as following:

i.   It takes two sentences S1 and S2 as its input.
ii. It creates a word set using the two sentences.
iii. It creates a semantic vector for each of the two sentences.
iv. It creates a word order vector for each of the two sentences.
v.   It uses the content word expansion (CWE) method to expand the words in the query and the sentence. Steps 3 and 4 employ this method to create the semantic vector and word order vector.

23

vi. It computes the semantic similarity measure between two sentences. The semantic similarity measure is determined by the cosine between the two corresponding semantic vectors.

vii. It calculates the word order similarity measure between two sentences. The similarity score is determined by the syntactic vector approach.

viii. Finally, it calculates the similarity measure between two sentences (S1 and S2) using a linear equation that combines the obtained similarity measures from steps 6 and 7.

ix. The final score obtained from the previous step is assigned to the edge between two sentences S1 and S2(Abdi et al. 2017).

d. K-Nearest Neighbor

This paper proposes a KNN algorithm where the similarity between the feature vectors is computed by considering the similarity feature as well as one among values.The process of applying the KNN to the text summarization which is mapped into a classification. The text is given as the input, and the classifier which corresponds to the subgroup which is most similar to the given text with respect to its content is selected. The text is partitioned into paragraphs, and each paragraph is classified into 'summary' or 'No summary' by the classifier. The paragraphs which are classified into 'summary' are extracted as results from summarizing the text. Note that the text is rejected, if all paragraphs are classified into 'remaining'. It works on feature and its numerical value so deep analysis of features and its values are required. KNN is a lazy algorithm(Jo 2017).

d. Linear combination of feature values

The number of features is extracted from the sentences and scores are assigned based on its feature values. Then the high ranked sentences are selected to be present in the summary. To query relevant sentences, the feature set is enriched with a number of other appropriate features(Afsharizadeh 2018).

2.2 Discussion

The focus of this research work is to discuss machine learning techniques for query-based text summarization. The different techniques being discussed on the basis of this study.

In Text Summarization, the summaries are generated as a general summary that highlights relevant information from the original document whereas query-based text summarization systems generate summaries contains related information to the user query. The difference between query and document of length. The document can be comprised of one word while a query is a special kind of document have a specific length. The techniques being discussed below:

2.2.1 Probabilistic Models:

These models are also named as statistical models or Language Modeling Methods. These include a repetitive process that makes predictions about frequencies of interesting and ranking document d according to the query q. The problem with such models is that they give zero probabilities to the non-existing word in both query and document which leads towards the inaccuracy. But with the passage of time the work in this area being done to improve these techniques which are known as smoothing techniques. Smoothing techniques use Bayesian Algorithm in such a way that it gives some probability between 0 and 1 to the unseen words rather than 0 and named models as Query likelihood Models for Query-Based Text Summarization that works on Relevance score by counting exact words between query and document. Query Likelihood is a Relevance Model in which document can be rank against the query where the probability of a document is interpreted as the Likelihood which predicts the relevancy between the documents and query. This shows the probabilistic score that how much query tokens and sentence of documents are relevant to each other. The selection of Smoothing techniques is very important for Query likelihood Model to achieve accuracy. Some of the smoothing techniques used with the model are as follow (Zhai and Lafferty 2001):

Dirichlet prior: - It works well on short queries.

Jelinek-Mercer method: - It works well on long queries.

Maximum Likelihood: - It takes the highest possible likelihood to the observations.

2.2.2 Linguistic Models:

They are knowledge-based models that having learning capability using Natural Language Processing concepts (Abdi et al. 2017). Lesk model is based on word ambiguity and give back synonym on the base of probabilistic generated result. It is used for semantic matching by using Lexical Dictionary (Basile, Caputo, and Semeraro 2014) where Jaccard Coefficient contains the count of exact word match among query and each individual sentence of the documents. It uses Union of all matching word between the query and sentence divided by intersection always return the score between 0 to 1. if two sentences have same token matching to the query have different length, Higher rank will be given to sentence have shorter length against query but all token must be matched to the query (Achananuparp et al. 2008). The Vector Space Model determines the similarity angle between the query and each individual sentence in the document using the Vector Space Model. In this mode, the TF-IDF Algorithm is used in which query and sentence of the document are represented as a vector in vector space and return the angle between the sentence and query vector. As Cosine similarity uses the trigonometric function cosine. According to cosine principle, the value of cosine will always lie in between -1 and 1. If the angle approaches towards 1 this means this vector (query token and document or sentence) have higher similarity otherwise if the value approaches towards -1 means the vector (query token and document or sentence) have very low similarity. If cosine angle is exactly "0" mean there is no angle between the vector (query token and document/sentence) mean they have no Document and query have any similarity. This   Algorithm of vector space model consists of two portions. 1st is TF (Term Frequency) and 2nd IDF (Inverse of Document Frequency). 1st it will calculate the dot product of TF.IDF of query and document and 2nd Divide by the dot product of magnitude (TF.IDF) of the query and (TF.IDF) of document (Siva Kumar, Premchand, and Govardhan 2011).

2.2.3 Supervised and Unsupervised models: learning models are termed as supervised learning whereas clustering termed as unsupervised learning models. In supervised learning, labels are known wherein unsupervised learning labels are unknown on the basis of feature and techniques the labels are decided. Graphs and decision tree models can be supervised as well as unsupervised. These techniques work on the basis of features extracted between query Q and document Features plays an important role for better results. Mostly these days' graphs and linear models are being used such as Support Vector Machine (SVM), Support Vector Regression (SVR). In these models the features being identified from the given query and a document. The relevant information according to the query being retrieved. Sentences or passages within the document must be identified. This is referred to as the sentence selection problem. After the relevant sentences have been identified, the composition Phase begins. When composing an abstract, it is important to consider how many sentences to include, and how to compress the sentences to fit within a fixed bounding box. The machine learning techniques used to solve the sentence selection problem. There are several benefits to using such techniques. First, they provide an easy means of incorporating a wide range of features. Second, depending on the machine learning technique used, the model can be learned over a rich function space. The features are divided into two categories. Query-dependent feature attempt to capture how relevant a given sentence S is to the query Q. These include an exact match, Overlap, Overlap-synonyms. Query-Independent feature goal is to encode any prior knowledge we have about individual sentences i.e. sentence length, sentence location. Identification of proper feature set feature sets available as the mark so that other researchers can develop and evaluate. Learning to rank techniques for the sentence selection task which has very different characteristics than the typical ad-hoc and web retrieval tasks (Metzler and Kanungo 2008). Semantic Graph, document graph for query-based summarization in which a combination of semantic relations between words and their syntactic composition is analyzed to extract meaningful sentences from document sets. The method is executed by computing the semantic and syntactic similarity of the sentence-to-sentence and sentence- to-query. To reduce redundancy in summary, this method uses the greedy algorithm to impose diversity penalty on the sentences. In addition, the proposed method expands the words in both the query and the sentences to tackle the problem of information limit. The graph computation is done in two steps first the document graph is created in which in which the document is parsed and split it into text fragments using a delimiter that includes a newline character. Each text fragments becomes a node in the document graph. A weighted edge is added to the document graph between two nodes if they either correspond to adjacent text fragments in the text or if they are semantically related, and the weight of an edge denotes the degree of the relationship. After this, the query is being processed on the graph. Artificial Neural Networks are also a kind of graph that can be processed by applying learning techniques or unsupervised techniques. Cluster-ordering algorithm orders clusters based on the cluster importance, which is computed by the sum of the weights of the content words of a cluster. The importance of a cluster based on the number of important words it contains. a Summing up the discussion the supervised and unsupervised models are used combined in a hybrid way with the linguistic models and statistical models. The linguistic and statistical model only focuses on a single attribute that is word count only in the different way but supervised and unsupervised models make analysis in a different perspective to lead toward accuracy. In such models, the feature extraction helps to make a strong decision and the linguistic and statistical techniques may act as a feature for the SVR KNN ANN and many other algorithms that help to achieve results near to accuracy. For example, as one of the query-dependent feature relevance score feature so to extract this feature the statistical algorithms being used and so on so the algorithms and techniques may act as a feature for the supervised n unsupervised algorithm and these days many researchers are being worked to introduce such hybrid techniques.

Chapter 3

Methodology

In this section the methodology of the research being discussed. The first step is to convert non-structure data into structure data by removing noise from both the text document as well as from the entered user query. The second step is to extract the features of query and document that gives best and accurate retrieval.

3.1 Preprocessing

In information retrieval system the data or information can be only possible to retrieve from a database or another system pure only if data is already in the structure form. Otherwise, data has to be passed through the preprocessing step which brings the unstructured data to structured data.

In text mining, the unstructured data include capitalization i.e tokens in the upper case should be converted to lower case because user query mostly included lower case word. The matching of tokens in the collection of documents is easy to find a match. It also included no stemming, lemmatization and stop words within the collection of documents. The removal of these from the text in information retrieval is important otherwise the information retrieved from the system. The noise may retrieve irrelevant information to the user requirement.

The NLP techniques are applied for preprocessing to convert structured data into the structured data. In this research, the preprocessing of text is performed in two steps. These are as follow

1. Noise Removal

2. Word normalization

3.1.1 Noise Removal

Noise in the document means "irrelevant or meaningless" data, therefore, noise removal is one of the steps of the preprocessing process. No chance for such words to become a parameter of query and document to retrieve user-required information from the collections of documents. Noise Removal includes Stop word removal and Word boundaries (Morgan and Garigl 2015).

3.1.2 Stop Word Removal

The most frequent word often does not carry meaning like "the, a, of, an, in etc." during the retrieval of information from the document. These words are not included in any document or sentence while giving a score to sentence or document for ranking. Like for example counting word in the sentence for finding sentence length, these words can't be included. Stopword list which is used in this Research is "*an all, an, and, any, are, as, be, be, but, by, few, for, have, he, her, here, him, his, how, I, in, is, it, its, many, me, me, none, of, on, or, our, she, some, the, their, them, there, they, that, this, us, was, what, when, where, which, who, why, will, with, you, your* " these are list of words which are removed from question as well as Corpus. In Retrieval both "question and corpus" documents must be free from such words otherwise it will increase the ambiguities.

3.1.3 Word boundaries

Word boundaries have the same level of effect as a stop word, but word boundaries are not any word. It includes white space and punctuation marks and abbreviation like for instance: - ".",",",","?". It is never considered as part of sentence length or sentence or documents score.

3.1.4 Word Normalization

Word Normalization is a process that converts a list of words to a more uniform sequence(Manning, Ragahvan, and Schutze 2009). Word Normalization is useful in preparing text for processing against the query. By transforming the words into a standard format. The other operations are able to work with the data and will not have to deal with issues that might compromise the process. The word normalization includes (Morgan and Garigl 2015).

a. Tokenization

It describes splitting paragraphs into sentences, or sentences into individual words. Sentences can be split into individual words through a similar process. Most commonly this split across white spaces(Manning, Ragahvan, and Schutze 2009) (Morgan and Garigl 2015). Open NLP Tokenizes "Simple Tokenizes" is used which is good to split the English avoiding including the white space consider as a token string. The split can be also used for tokenizing but the result of this sometimes that we have faced already it includes white space to be count in the sentence length. Another hand, Simple tokenizer is simple and gives correct splitting of the sentence into tokens but it only works on English. For Other Languages like Roman Urdu where there is no standard structure of language where uses of English with other languages is common, so it can be batter split by using String. Split ().

b. Stemming

Stemming is a process where words are reduced to root by removing inflection through dropping unnecessary characters, usually a suffix(Manning, Ragahvan, and Schutze 2009). Finding the Stem of a word involves removing any prefixes or suffixes and what is left is considered to be the stem or root. Identifying stems is useful tasks where finding the similar word is important. For example, a search maybe looking for occurrences of word likes "boo". There are many words that contain this word including books, booked, bookings, and bookmark. It can be useful to identify stems and then look for their occurrences in a document. Many situations, this can improve the quality of a search (Manning, Ragahvan, and Schutze 2009)

c. Lemmatization

It is an alternative approach from stemming to removing inflection. By determining the part of speech and utilizing WorldNet's lexical database of English, Lemmatization can get better results. Lemmatization is a more intensive and therefore slower process, but more accurate (Manning, Ragahvan, and Schutze 2009). Similar to Stemming is Lemmatization. This is the process of finding its lemma, its form as found in a dictionary. This can also be useful for some searches. Stemming is frequently viewed as a more primitive technique, where the attempt to get to the "root" of a word involves cutting off parts of the beginning and/or ending of a token(Morgan and Garigl 2015). Lemmatization can be thought of as a more sophisticated approach where effort is devoted to finding the morphological or vocabulary meaning of a token. For example, the word "having "has a stem of "have" while its lemma is "had". Also, the words "was" and "been" have different stems but the same lemma, "be"(Morgan and Garigl 2015).

d. Remove Capitalization

The text often has a variety of capitalization reflecting the beginning of sentences, proper nouns emphasis. The most common approach is to reduce everything to lower case for simplicity(Morgan and Garigl 2015). When using Name Entity Recognition of Stanford University API, the Capitalization should not be removed because document Carpus and Question may lose the Name Entity because of Removing Capitalization. The solution to this problem is Removing Capitalization process should take place after when Name Entity is recognizing and extracted from documents carpus and question.

3.2 Features Extraction and Analysis

Converting text data into numerical data. Machines can't understand the textual data, so it needed to be converted into numerical form so for this purpose the feature extraction process has been taken using different machine learning algorithms to extract the answer from the document according to the user query/question. In this research, some query dependent and some query independent features are considered that have a high impact on the output.

3.2.1 Query-dependent Feature

Query-dependent features are those features whose scores, or values are calculated among the query and each individual sentence in the document. These features are as follow:

a. Word Match Feature

To extract this feature Jaccard coefficient similarity algorithm is used. This feature contains the count of exact word match among query and each individual sentence of the documents. It uses Union of all matching word between the query and sentence divided by intersection always return the score between 0 to 1. If two sentences have same token matching to the query have different length, the higher rank will be given to sentence have shorter length against the query, but all token must be matched to the query. The equation is given below (Achananuparp et al. 2008).

$$\text{Jaccard Similarity } J(A,B) = | \text{ Intersection }(A,B)\ |\ /\ |\ \text{Union }(A,B)\ | \qquad \text{Eq 3.1}$$

b. Semantic word match feature

It works is based on checking similarity ambiguity and give back synonym on the base of probabilistic generated result. The condition in our program if we have greater probability i.e. 0.5 Then derived synonym word from our dictionary will be selected as a matched token which will increase the score of sentences against the query. For this purpose, we use word Net Dictionary which works using word Net is a database of English. Where it has grouped Nouns, verbs, adjectives, and adverbs into sets of cognitive synonyms each expressing a distinct concept.

c. Name Entity score

It recognizes name entities (person and company names, etc.). it uses annotator class to identify the label against the entity. This annotator uses machine learning sequence model to label entities, but it may also call specialist rule-based component, such as for labeling and interpreting time and date. This annotator recognizes the name (Person, location, organization, music), in numeric (Money, Number, Ordinal, Percent) and Temporal (Date, time, Duration, Set). We used Stanford NER Classifier I.E four class classifier which recognizes the name (Person location, organization, Misc. between the query and each individual sentence in the document). For this classifier, we need our question and sentence in having entities in original capital form(Manning, Ragahvan, and Schutze 2009).

d. TF-weightage score

This feature is used for extracting the similarity angle between the query and each individual sentence in the document using the Vector Space Model. In this mode, the TF-IDF Algorithm is used in which query and sentence of the document are represented as a vector in vector space and return the angle between the sentence and query vector. As Cosine similarity uses the trigonometric function cosine. According to cosine principle, the value of cosine will always lie in between -1 and 1. If the angle approaches towards 1 this means this vector (query token and document or sentence) have higher similarity otherwise if the value approaches towards -1 means the vector (query token and document or sentence) have very low similarity. If cosine angle is exactly "0" mean there is no angle between the vector (query token and document/sentence) mean they have no Document and query have any similarity. This   Algorithm of vector space model consists of two portions. 1st is TF (Term Frequency) and 2nd IDF (Inverse of Document Frequency). 1st it will calculate the dot product of TF.IDF of query and document and 2nd Divide by the dot product of magnitude (TF.IDF) of the query and (TF.IDF) of the document.The general equation is given below. If a single token of the query is not found in the document the total score against the query for current documents or sentence will result in exactly 0.

$$\text{similarity} = \cos(\theta) = \frac{\mathbf{A} \cdot \mathbf{B}}{\|\mathbf{A}\| \|\mathbf{B}\|} = \frac{\sum_{i=1}^{n} A_i B_i}{\sqrt{\sum_{i=1}^{n} A_i^2} \sqrt{\sum_{i=1}^{n} B_i^2}} \qquad \text{Eq 3.2}$$

e. Relevance Score

Using Query Likelihood Relevance Model Algorithm (Zhai and Lafferty 2001) document can be rank against the query where the probability of a document is interpreted as the Likelihood. It predicts the relevancy between the document and query? Which shows the probabilistic score that how much query tokens and sentence of documents are relevant to each other? Means the more we have a token matching pair of tokens with document/sentence the more we will have similarity probability score against the query.

$$f_{JM}(q, d) = \sum_{\substack{w \in d \\ w \in q}} c(w, q) \log \left(1 + \frac{1 - \lambda}{\lambda} \frac{c(w, d)}{|d| p(w|C)} \right) \qquad \text{Eq 3.3}$$

3.2.2 Query independent Feature

a. Stop word count

In this feature, the total stop word contained in each individual sentence is count by counting the no of tokens that containing the stop words. For this purpose, first, the whole document is converted into tokens by the help of tokenization process and then each token is compared with the list of stop word if a token contains stop word then it will have counted otherwise the token is ignored. (Ouyang et al. 2010)

b. Named entity analysis/ independent

Recognizes named entities (person and company names, etc.) in the text. Principally, this annotator uses one or more machine learning sequence models to label entities, but it may also call specialist rule-based components, such as for labeling and interpreting times and dates. This annotator recognizes named (PERSON, LOCATION, ORGANIZATION,

35

MISC), numerical (MONEY, NUMBER, ORDINAL, PERCENT), and temporal (DATE, TIME, DURATION, SET). We used standard ford ner classifier i.e. four class classifier that recognizes named (PERSON, LOCATION, ORGANIZATION, MISC) in each individual sentence in the document(Ouyang et al. 2010).

c. TF-Weightage

TF-IDF stands for term frequency-inverse document frequency, and the TF-IDF weight is a weight often used in information retrieval and text mining. This weight is a statistical measure used to evaluate how important a word is to a document in a collection or corpus (Ouyang et al. 2010).

d. Sentence position:

opening sentences are more informative and more important to the document set thus define the position-based feature (Ouyang et al. 2010).

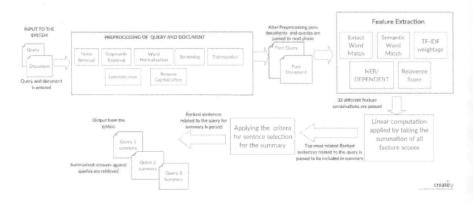

Figure 3.1 Methodology for Feature Analysis

Chapter 4
Results

Feature selection in data mining, Text Mining, and Machine Learning is an essential task. The features play an important role to retrieve correct and related output(Metzler and Kanungo 2008). The identification of the features and the analysis of its impact on accuracy is also an essential step in the text summarization or information retrieval(Zhao et al. 2008). The work of this research focused on the combination of such features that leads to accuracy. The feature analysis of text document or query the NLP techniques and concepts are required to understand the importance of each individual word. In the text document or corpus, the properties or characteristic are different in different perspective. The analysis of query dependent features is performed on the following questions. The table below shows the question and their answers.

Table 4.1 Results

S. No	Questions	Possible Answers
Q#1	What is an earth year?	**Sentence no: 38** Earth revolves around the Sun in 365.26 days, a period is known as an Earth year. **Sentence no: 68** An Earth year is the time it takes the earth to make one orbit of the sun
Q#2	Where has William Shakespeare born?	**Sentence no: 0** William Shakespeare (baptized on April 26, 1564, to April 23, 1616) was an English

		playwright, actor, and poet also known as the "Bard of Avon" and often called England's national poet. **Sentence no: 1** Born in Stratford-upon-Avon, England, he was an important member of the Lord Chamberlain's Men company of theatrical players from roughly 1594 onward.
Q#3	How does flamingos nest look like?	**Sentence no: 33** Flamingos build nests that look like mounds of mud along waterways.
Q#4	When Google was founded?	**Sentence no: 26** Google was founded in 1998 by Larry Page and Sergey Brin while they were Ph.D. students at Stanford University, California **Sentence no: 27** they incorporated Google as a privately held company on September 4, 1998
Q#5	What is machine learning?	**Sentence no: 43** Machine learning is a field of computer science that gives computer systems the ability to "learn" (i.e. **Sentence no: 103** Machine perception deals with the capability to use sensory inputs to deduce the different aspects of the world, while computer vision is the power to analyze visual inputs with a few sub-problems such as facial, object and gesture recognition.

		Sentence no: 45 Machine learning is closely related to (and often overlaps with) computational statistics, which also focuses on prediction-making through the use of computers.
Q#6	What are the challenges in natural language processing frequently involves?	**Sentence no: 5** Challenges in natural-language processing frequently involve speech recognition, natural-language understanding, and natural-language generation.
Q#7	How long earth has been formed?	**Sentence no: 36** According to radiometric dating and other sources of evidence, Earth formed over 4 billion years ago
Q#8	What is the official language of Pakistan?	The answer is not in the document so retrieve any related sentence according to Pakistan or any other.
Q#9	Why we use data mining techniques?	**Sentence no: 54** Machine learning is a field of computer science that uses statistical techniques to give computer systems the ability to "learn" (i.e., progressively improve performance on a specific task) with data, without being explicitly programmed. **Sentence no: 47** Machine learning is sometimes conflated with data mining, where the latter subfield focuses more on exploratory data analysis and is known as unsupervised learning

Q#10	What are the main aspects of life in the plays of Shakespeare?	**Sentence no: 3** All that can be deduced is that, in his 20 years as a playwright, Shakespeare wrote plays that capture the complete range of human emotion and conflict.
Q#11	Where Quaid-e-Azam Muhammad Ali Jinnah did get his education?	**sentence no: 19** Quaid-e-Azam Born on December 25, 1876, in a prominent mercantile family in Karachi and educated at the Sindh Madrassa-ul-Islam and the Christian Mission School at his birthplace, Jinnah joined the Lincoln's Inn in 1893 to become the youngest Indian to be called to the Bar, three years later
Q#12	What is robotics?	**Sentence no: 73** Robotics is a branch of engineering that involves the conception, design, manufacture, and operation of robots. **Sentence no:71** Robotics is an interdisciplinary branch of engineering and science that includes mechanical engineering, electrical engineering, computer science, and others. **Sentence no: 72** Robotics deals with the design, construction, operation, and use of robots, as well as computer systems for their control, sensory feedback, and information processing. **Sentence no: 80**

		Many of today's robots are inspired by nature, contributing to the field of bio-inspired robotics
Q#13	What is the importance of robotics?	**Sentence no: 73** Robotics is a branch of engineering that involves the conception, design, manufacture, and operation of robots. **Sentence no: 71** Robotics is an interdisciplinary branch of engineering and science that includes mechanical engineering, electrical engineering, computer science, and others. **Sentence no: 72** Robotics deals with the design, construction, operation, and use of robots, as well as computer systems for their control, sensory feedback, and information processing. **Sentence no: 80** Many of today's robots are inspired by nature, contributing to the field of bio-inspired robotics
Q#14	What is meant by ocean tides?	**Sentence no: 41** The interaction between the Earth and Moon causes ocean tides, stabilizes the Earth's orientation on its axis, and gradually slows its rotation.
Q#15	What is angiosperm?	**Sentence no: 63** A reproductive structure in angiosperms (flowering plants), often conspicuously colorful and typically including sepals, petals, and either or both stamens and/or a Pistil is called the

		flower
Q#16	What is the result of ethnic civil war in 1971?	**sentence no: 10** An ethnic civil war in 1971 resulted in the secession of East Pakistan as the new country of Bangladesh.
Q#17	What is the services apple providing to its users?	**sentence no: 60** Apple was founded in 1976 by Steve Jobs, Steve Wozniak, and Ronald Wayne, Apple is best known for making some of the world's most ubiquitous consumer devices, software, and services: the iPhone, iPad, iMac and MacBook computers, Apple TV, Apple Watch, iOS, iCloud, iTunes, Apple Music, Apple Pay, and many more.
Q#18	What happened in 1976?	**Sentence no: 52** Apple was founded by Steve Jobs, Steve Wozniak, and Ronald Wayne in April 1976 to develop and sell Wozniak's Apple I personal computer. **sentence no: 61** Apple was founded in 1976 by Steve Jobs, Steve Wozniak, and Ronald Wayne, Apple is best known for making some of the world's most ubiquitous consumer devices, software, and services: the iPhone, iPad, iMac and MacBook computers, Apple TV, Apple Watch, iOS, iCloud, iTunes, Apple Music, Apple Pay, and many more.

Q#19	How many times does the earth rotate around its axis?	**Sentence no: 39** During this time, Earth rotates about its axis about 366.26 times.
Q#20	When was Pakistan created?	**Sentence no: 7** As a result of the Pakistan Movement led by Muhammad Ali Jinnah and the subcontinent's struggle for independence, Pakistan was created in 1947 as an independent homeland for Indian Muslims.

In this research, a single doc file is acting as corpus having unrelated data. The available answer in query consider as YES and for those queries, the answer is not mentioned in corpus consider as NO. The above questions are tested on the corpus to visualize the impact of Query Dependent features. The analysis is performed to identify such set of queries dependent feature that has high retrieval accuracy.

4.1 Query Dependent Feature Analysis

Query-dependent features attempt to capture how relevant a given sentence S is to the query Q (Metzler and Kanungo 2008). (Metzler and Kanungo 2008) (Achananuparp, Hu, and Shen 2008) (Ouyang et al. 2010). According to NLP, the English words have many properties which lead to extract the sentence from the document according to the user query (Kaur 2017). In research we first checked the impact of each property individually then we make 32 different combinations of the features to analysis that which set of feature combination leads us to accuracy by using linear approach by taking the summation of the feature score. The following final set of features as mention below

Exact word match +Word Disambiguity sense+ Term frequency +relevance score+ NER/D

43

The value of each and the individual feature is obtained between the query and each individual sentence of the document. And then the sentence is ranked upon the score from highest score to lowest score. **The threshold of our approach is the first five ranked sentences against each query**. The observation is taken upon the following Criteria:

Criteria 1: The query related answer must be at the 1st position.

Criteria 2: The first five ranked sentences must have related to the topic of the user's query.

Criteria 3: The related answer for the user query must at any top 5 positions.

Table 4.2 Ranked Sentences

QUESTION NO	SEQUENCES				
	SENTENCE 5	SENTENCE 4	SENTENCE 3	SENTECNE 2	SENTEN CE 1
Q#1 what is earth year?	41	37	36	68	38
Q# 2 Where William Shakespeare born?	3	1	2	64	0
Q#3 How Flamingo nest looks like?	30	96	58	31	33
Q#4 When Google was founded?	90	28	53	61	26

Q# 5 What is Machine learning?	45	102	43	55	99
Q#6 What are challenges in NLP frequently involve?	71	72	36	4	5
Q#7 How long Earth has been formed?	37	40	68	41	36
Q#8 What is the official language of Pakistan?	6	4	10	11	9
Q#9 Why we use data mining techniques?	75	76	65	47	54
Q#10 What are the main aspects of Shakespeare in his plays?	103	2	92	70	3
Q#11 Where did Quaid e Azam Muhammad Ali	21	79	19	20	7

Jinnah get an education?					
Q#12 What is Robotics?	82	72	71	73	80
Q# 13 What is the importance of Robotics?	82	72	71	73	80
Q# 14 What is meant by Ocean tides?	33	32	31	66	41
Q#15 What is Angiosperm?	14	13	18	12	63
Q# 16 What was the result of ethnic civil war in 9171?	12	6	0	7	10
Q# 17 What are the services apple providing to its user?	52	60	51	48	12
Q#18 What happened in 1976?	2	1	0	61	52
Q# 20 When Pakistan was created?	1	9	11	7	6

4.1.1 Confusion Matrix for the selected combination of Query Dependent features

Answer of 19 queries are available in the document classified as =TP (True Positive)

Answer of 1 query is not available in the document as classified as= TN (True Negative)

If criteria are fulfilled=CORRECT

If criteria are not fulfilled=WRONG

N=total no of queries=20

Table 4.3 Criteria 1 Analysis

	Predicted wrong	Predicted correct	
Actual wrong	TN=1	FP=5	6
Actual correct	FN=0	TP=14	19
	1	19	

Table 4.4 Criteria 2 Analysis

	Predicted wrong	Predicted correct	
Actual wrong	TN=1	FP=8	9
Actual correct	FN=0	TP=11	11
	1	19	

Table 4.5 Criteria 3 Analysis

	Predicted wrong	Predicted correct	
Actual wrong	TN=1	FP=0	1
Actual correct	FN=0	TP=19	11

	1	19	

Table 4.6 Evalutaion Measures for criterias

Criteria	EVALUATION CRITERIA			
	Accuracy	Error Rate	Precision	Prevalence
Criteria 1	75%	25%	73.68%	95%
Criteria 2	60%	40%	57.89%	55%
Criteria 3	100%	0%	100%	95%

Chapter 5

Comparative analysis of Query Likelihood Model and Vector Space Model

According to this research compared the accuracy reveals that the results of Query likelihood have higher accuracy rate as compare to the vector space model. The reason behind this is the product TF of searching word having zero scores if not found in the document. This zero-product problem can be resolved by smoothing. On the other side, the query likelihood hood uses a smoothing technique to overcome this issue by assigning 1 against any searching token in the query. In the experimental setup, we have shown the result to reveal this issue where it shows the query likelihood has higher accuracy than the vector space model shown in Table 5.2.

5.1 Experimental Setup:

This experiment is performed by putting 20 quires against a single document which included 20 different paragraphs having a different topic discussion and each paragraph have multiple sentences the score against any query always assign to sentences in a paragraph. The higher the score of the sentence related to any paragraph is ranked finally to show how much the top sentences are related against the query.

5.1.1 Dataset

This experiment has a single document having different paragraph having total 105 sentences.

5.1.2 Language tool:

The experiment is performed using Java as a programming language.

5.1.3 Queries

The queries used in this experiment for testing the performance of these algorithms shown in Table 4.1

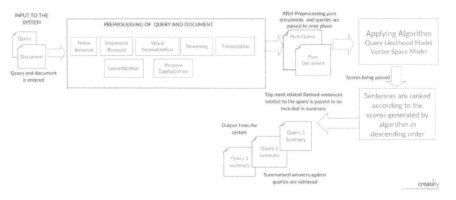

Figure 5.1 Methodology for Comparative Analysis

In this experiment, both algorithms are applied to the same document and queries in order to compare the performance of algorithms on the basis of the accuracy of most related possible answers. The algorithm gives output in the form of numerical value considered as a score of sentences against each sentence. The scores are ordered in descending order and then the top-ranked sentence being selected as the answer for the query. The vector space model predict correct answers for 10 queries out of 20 queries whereas Query likelihood Model predicts 16 correct answers for the queries because in vector space model the tf of single word is zero the whole result becomes zero due to the dot product between query word and document word but due to Smoothing techniques it gives some probability between 0 and 1 to the unseen words rather than 0. Due to the limitation in the vector space model the accuracy of this algorithm is less than the query likelihood model. The predicted answer against each query is mentioned in the given table.

Table 5.1 Testing Results of Algorithms

Query No	Sentence predicted by Vector space Model	Prediction	Sentence predicted by Query likelihood Model	Prediction
Q#1	Sentence no: 36 According to radiometric dating and other sources of evidence, Earth formed over 4 billion years ago.	Wrong	Sentence no: 38 Earth revolves around the Sun in 365.26 days, a period is known as an Earth year.	Correct
Q#2	Sentence no: 0 William Shakespeare (baptized on April 26, 1564, to April 23, 1616) was an English playwright, actor, and poet also known as the "Bard of Avon" and often called England's national poet.	Correct	sentence no: 0 William Shakespeare (baptized on April 26, 1564, to April 23, 1616) was an English playwright, actor, and poet also known as the "Bard of Avon" and often called England's national poet	Correct
Q#3	Sentence no: 33 Flamingos build nests that look like mounds of mud along waterways.	Correct	Sentence no: 33 Flamingos build nests that look like mounds of mud along waterways.	Correct

Q#4	Sentence no: 26 Google was founded in 1998 by Larry Page and Sergey Brin while they were Ph.D. students at Stanford University, California	Correct	Sentence no: 26 Google was founded in 1998 by Larry Page and Sergey Brin while they were Ph.D. students at Stanford University, California	correct
Q#5	Sentence no: 55 The name machine learning was coined in 1959 by Arthur Samuel.	Wrong	Sentence no: 99 Machine learning is another core part of AI.	Wrong
Q#6	Sentence no: 5 Challenges in natural-language processing frequently involve speech recognition, natural-language understanding, and natural-language generation.	Correct	Sentence no: 5 Challenges in natural-language processing frequently involve speech recognition, natural-language understanding, and natural-language generation.	Correct
Q#7	sentence no : 0 William Shakespeare (baptized on April 26, 1564, to April 23, 1616) was an English playwright, actor, and	Wrong	Sentence no: 36 According to radiometric dating and other sources of evidence, Earth formed over 4 billion	Correct

	poet also known as the "Bard of Avon" and often called England's national poet		years ago.	
Q#8	Answer not mention it retrieve any sentence randomly	Correct	Answer not mention it retrieve any sentence randomly	Correct
Q#10	**Sentence no: 3** all that can be deduced is that, in his 20 years as a playwright, Shakespeare wrote plays that capture the complete range of human emotion and conflict.	Correct	**Sentence no: 3** all that can be deduced is that, in his 20 years as a playwright, Shakespeare wrote plays that capture the complete range of human emotion and conflict.	Correct
Q#11	**sentence no: 0** William Shakespeare (baptized on April 26, 1564, to April 23, 1616) was an English playwright, actor, and poet also known as the "Bard of Avon" and often called England's national poet	Wrong	**sentence no: 7** As a result of Pakistan Movement led by Muhammad Ali Jinnah and the subcontinent's struggle for Independence, Pakistan was created in 1947 as an independent homeland for Indian Muslims.	Wrong
Q#12	**Sentence no: 71** Robotics is an interdisciplinary branch	Correct	**Sentence no: 80** Many of today's robots are inspired by	Correct

	of engineering and science that includes mechanical engineering, electrical engineering, computer science, and others.		nature, contributing to the field of bio-inspired robotics	
Q#13	**Sentence no: 0** William Shakespeare (baptized on April 26, 1564, to April 23, 1616) was an English playwright, actor, and poet also known as the "Bard of Avon" and often called England's national poet.	Wrong	**Sentence no: 80** Many of today's robots are inspired by nature, contributing to the field of bio-inspired robotics	Correct
Q#14	**Sentence no: 0** William Shakespeare (baptized on April 26, 1564, to April 23, 1616) was an English playwright, actor, and poet also known as the "Bard of Avon" and often called England's national poet.	Wrong	**Sentence no: 41** The interaction between the Earth and Moon causes ocean tides, stabilizes the Earth's orientation on its axis, and gradually slows its rotation	Correct
Q#15	**Sentence no: 12** A flowers, sometimes	Correct	**Sentence no: 12** A flowers, sometimes	Correct

	known as a bloom or blossom, is the reproductive structure found in flowering plants (plants of the division Magnoliophyte, also called angiosperms).		known as a bloom or blossom, is the reproductive structure found in flowering plants (plants of the division Magnoliophyte, also called angiosperms).	
Q#16	**sentence no: 10** An ethnic civil war in 1971 resulted in the secession of East Pakistan as the new country of Bangladesh	Correct	**sentence no: 10** An ethnic civil war in 1971 resulted in the secession of East Pakistan as the new country of Bangladesh	Correct
Q#18	**sentence no: 0** William Shakespeare (baptized on April 26, 1564, to April 23, 1616) was an English playwright, actor, and poet also known as the "Bard of Avon" and often called England's national poet	Wrong	**Sentence no: 52** Apple was founded by Steve Jobs, Steve Wozniak, and Ronald Wayne in April 1976 to develop and sell Wozniak's Apple I personal computer.	Correct
Q#19	**Sentence no: 39** During this time, Earth rotates about its axis	Correct	**Sentence no: 39** During this time, Earth rotates about its	Correct

	about 366.26 times.		axis about 366.26 times.	
Q#20	**Sentence no: 6** Pakistan is unique among Muslim countries in that it is the only country to have been created in the name of Islam.	Wrong	**Sentence no: 7** As a result of the Pakistan Movement led by Muhammad Ali Jinnah and the subcontinent's struggle for independence, Pakistan was created in 1947 as an independent homeland for Indian Muslims.	Correct

5.2 Results of Comparative Analysis:

The overall predicted answer for vector space model against queries shows 55% accuracy having 11 correct predicted answers and 9 wrong predicted answers. On the other hand, for Query likelihood, the predicted answer against queries shows 85% accuracy having 17 correct predicted answers and 3 wrong predicted answers shown in the given table.

Table 5.2 Accuracy of Algorithms

Algorithms	Total no of queries	Correct prediction	Wrong prediction	Accuracy for correct prediction
Vector space Model	20	11	9	(11/20) *100=55%

Query likelihood Model	20	17	3	(17/20) *100=85%

Chapter 6
Conclusion

The amount of data and information is increasing exponentially. The domain includes web as well as data of various organizations on their local servers. This forms basis for the data scientists to explore new techniques to fulfill market needs in the field of IR. This research work discusses machine learning techniques used for query-based text summarization. After extensive study of views of different data scientists and authors, it is concluded that a combination of supervised and unsupervised machine learning algorithm in order to apply linguistic and statistical techniques gives better results than a standalone single technique. The process improves the score of accurate feature extraction, reduces redundancy of calculations and identification of specified data according to query. The future work suggested is to apply the same hybrid techniques for Abstractive summarization on the basis of user queries. This will help to make the system efficient for linking files in digital archives system.

References

1. Abdi, Asad, Norisma Idris, Rasim M. Alguliyev, and Ramiz M. Aliguliyev. 2017. "Query-Based Multi-Documents Summarization Using Linguistic Knowledge and Content Word Expansion." *Springer* 21(7): 1785–1801.

2. Achananuparp, Palakorn, Xiaohua Hu, and Xiajiong Shen. 2008. "The Evaluation of Sentence Similarity Measures." : 305–16. http://cci.drexel.edu/faculty/thu/research-papers/dawak-547.pdf.

3. Achananuparp, Palakorn, Xiaohua Hu, Xiaohua Zhou, and Xiaodan Zhang. 2008. "Utilizing Sentence Similarity and Question Type Similarity to Response to Similar Questions in Knowledge-Sharing Community." *Proceedings of QAWeb 2008 Workshop* 214.

4. Afsharizadeh, Mahsa. 2018. "Query-Oriented Text Summarization Using Sentence Extraction Technique." *2018 4th International Conference on Web Research (ICWR)*: 128–32.

5. Asthana, Amit, Er Vagish Tiwari, Er M C Pandey, and Er Ankit Misra. 2017. "A Novel Architecture for Agent-Based Text Summarization." *Asian Journal of Applied Science and Technology (AJAST)* 1(5): 164–69.

6. Basile, Pierpaolo, Annalina Caputo, and Giovanni Semeraro. 2014. "An Enhanced Lesk Word Sense Disambiguation Algorithm through a Distributional Semantic Model." *Proceedings of the 25th International Conference on Computational Linguistics: Technical Papers (COLING 14)*: 1591–1600.

7. Damova, Mariana, and St Kliment. 2014. "Query-Based Summarization : A Survey." (November).

58

8. Das, D., and A. F. T. Martins. 2016. "A Survey on Automatic Text Summarization." *2016 International Conference on Circuit, Power and Computing Technologies [ICCPCT]*: 1–31.

9. Durrett, Greg et al. 2014. "Learning-Based Single-Document Summarization with Compression and Anaphoricity Constraints." *IEEE*.

10. El-Haj, Mahmoud O., and Bassam H. Hammo. 2008. "Evaluation of Query-Based Arabic Text Summarization System." In *2008 International Conference on Natural Language Processing and Knowledge Engineering, NLP-KE 2008,*

11. Fisher, S, and B Roark. 2006. "Query-Focused Summarization By Supervised Sentence Ranking and Skewed Word Distributions." *In Proceedings of the 6th Document Understanding Conferences. DUC.*

12. Fuentes, Maria, Enrique Alfonseca, and Horacio Rodr. 2007. "Support Vector Machines for Query-Focused Summarization Trained and Evaluated on Pyramid Data." *ACM* (June): 57–60.

13. Gupta, Virendra Kumar, and Tanveer J. Siddiqui. 2012. "Multi-Document Summarization Using Sentence Clustering." *4th International Conference on Intelligent Human-Computer Interaction: Advancing Technology for Humanity, IHCI 2012.*

14. Hasselqvist, Johan, Niklas Helmertz, and Mikael Kågebäck. 2017. "Query-Based Abstractive Summarization Using Neural Networks." http://arxiv.org/abs/1712.06100.

15. Jain, Harshal J, M S Bewoor, and S H Patil. 2012. "Context Sensitive Text Summarization Using K Means Clustering Algorithm." *International Journal of Soft Computing and Engineering* 2(2): 301–4.

16. Jaoua, Fatma Kallel, and Abdelmajid Ben Hamadou. 2008. "A Learning Technique to Determine Criteria for Multiple Document Summarization." : 121–26.

17. Jo, Taeho. 2017. "K Nearest Neighbor for Text Summarization Using Feature Similarity." *IEEE Transactions on Knowledge and Data Engineering*: 0–4.

18. Judith D.Schlesinger, Deborah J.Baker, Robert L.Donaway. 2011. "Using Document

Features and Statistical Modeling to Improve Query-Based Summarization."

19. Kaur, Gurvir. 2017. "Review on Text Classification by NLP Approaches with Machine Learning and Data Mining Approaches." 3: 767–71.

20. Km, Shivakumar, Amrita Vishwa, and Shivakumar Km. 2016. "Text Summarization Using Clustering Technique and SVM Technique SVM Technique." *International Journal of Applied Engineering Research* (May).

21. Ko, Youngjoong. 2012. "A Study of Term Weighting Schemes Using Class Information for Text Classification." *Proceedings of the 35th international ACM SIGIR conference on Research and development in information retrieval - SIGIR '12*: 1029. http://dl.acm.org/citation.cfm?doid=2348283.2348453.

22. Litvak, Marina. 2017. "Query-Based Summarization Using MDL Principle." : 22–31.

23. Manning, Christopher D., Prabhakar Raghavan, and Hinrich Schutze. 2009. "An Introduction to Information Retrieval." *Information Retrieval* (c): 1–18.

24. Metzler, Donald, and Tapas Kanungo. 2008. "Machine Learned Sentence Selection Strategies for Query-Biased Summarization." *Sigir Learning To Rank Workshop*. http://citeseerx.ist.psu.edu/viewdoc/summary?doi=10.1.1.168.1477.

25. Morgan, Richard, and Roberto Garigl. 2015. Endeavour *Natural Language Processing with JAVA*.

26. Ouyang, You, Wenjie Li, Sujian Li, and Qin Lu. 2010. "Applying Regression Models to Query-Focused Multi-Document Summarization." *Information Processing and Management* 47(2): 227–37. http://dx.doi.org/10.1016/j.ipm.2010.03.005.

27. Profile, Feature, Multi-document Summarization, and Sentence Extraction. 2010. "C Lustering and Feature Specific Sentence E Xtraction Based Summarization Of." *International journal of computer science & information Technology (IJCSIT)* 2(4): 99–111.

28. Rahman, Nazreena, and Bhogeswar Borah. 2015. "A Survey on Existing Extractive Techniques for Query-Based Text Summarization." In *2015 International Symposium on Advanced Computing and Communication (ISACC)*, IEEE, 98–102. http://ieeexplore.ieee.org/document/7377323/.

29. Sankarasubramaniam, Yogesh, Krishnan Ramanathan, and Subhankar Ghosh. 2014. "Text Summarization Using Wikipedia." *Information Processing and Management* 50(3): 443–61. http://dx.doi.org/10.1016/j.ipm.2014.02.001.

30. Sarkar, Kamal. 2009. "Sentence Clustering-Based Summarization of Multiple Text Documents." *TECHNIA – International Journal of Computing Science and Communication Technologies* 2(1): 974–3375.

31. Shen, Chao, and Tao Li. 2011. "Learning to Rank for Query-Focused Multi-Document Summarization." *Proceedings - IEEE International Conference on Data Mining, ICDM*: 626–34.

32. Siva Kumar, A.P, P Premchand, and A Govardhan. 2011. "Query-Based Summarizer Based on Similarity of Sentences and Word Frequency." *International Journal of Data Mining & Knowledge Management Process* 1(3): 1–12. http://www.aircconline.com/ijdkp/V1N3/1311ijdkp01.pdf.

33. Teng, Zhi, Ye Liu, Fuji Ren, and Seiji Tsuchiya. 2008. "Single Document Summarization Based on Local Topic Identification and Word Frequency." *7th Mexican International Conference on Artificial Intelligence - Proceedings of the Special Session, MICAI 2008*: 37–41.

34. Thomas, Justine Raju, Santosh Kumar Bharti, and Korra Sathya Babu. 2016. "Automatic Keyword Extraction for Text Summarization in E-Newspapers." *Proceedings of the International Conference on Informatics and Analytics - ICIA-16*: 1–8. http://dl.acm.org/citation.cfm?doid=2980258.2980442.

35. Ture, Ferhan, and Elizabeth Boschee. 2014. "Learning to Translate : A Query-Specific Combination Approach for Cross-Lingual Information Retrieval." *Emnlp*: 589–99.

36. Valizadeh, Mohammadreza, and Pavel Brazdil. 2015. "Exploring Actor–object Relationships for Query-Focused Multi-Document Summarization." *Soft Computing* 19(11): 3109–21.

37. Varadarajan, Ramakrishna, and Vagelis Hristidis. 2006. "A System for Query-Specific Document Summarization." *Proceedings of the 15th ACM international*

conference on Information and knowledge management - CIKM '06: 622. http://portal.acm.org/citation.cfm?doid=1183614.1183703.

38. Wan, Xiaojun. 2010. "Towards a Unified Approach to Simultaneous Single-Document and Multi-Document Summarizations." *Proceedings of the 23rd International Conference on Computational Linguistics* (August): 1137–45.

39. Wang, Lu, Hema Raghavan, Vittorio Castelli, et al. 2016. "A Sentence Compression Based Framework to Query-Focused Multi-Document Summarization." http://arxiv.org/abs/1606.07548.

40. Wang, Lu, Hema Raghavan, Claire Cardie, and Vittorio Castelli. 2016. "Query-Focused Opinion Summarization for Uscr-Generated Content." http://arxiv.org/abs/1606.05702.

41. Wang, Xiaodong, Bei Xu, and Hai Zhuge. 2016. "Automatic Question Answering Based on Single Document." *2016 12th International Conference on Semantics, Knowledge and Grids Automatic.*

42. Yadav, Chandra Shekhar, and Aditi Sharan. 2015. "Hybrid Approach for Single Text Document Summarization Using Statistical and Sentiment Features." *International Journal of Information Retrieval Research* 5(4): 46–70. http://services.igi-global.com/resolvedoi/resolve.aspx?doi=10.4018/IJIRR.2015100104.

43. Yousefi Azar, Mahmood, Kairit Sirts, Len Hamey, and Diego Mollá Aliod. 2015. "Query-Based Single Document Summarization Using an Ensemble Noisy Auto-Encoder." *Proceedings of the Australasian Language Technology Association Workshop*: 2–10.

44. Zhai, Chengxiang et al. 2008. "Single Document Summarization Based on Local Topic Identification and Word Frequency." *Proceedings of the 24th annual international ACM SIGIR conference on Research and development in information retrieval - SIGIR '01* 18(June): 304–19. http://cci.drexel.edu/faculty/thu/research-papers/dawak-547.pdf.

45. Zhai, Chengxiang, and John Lafferty. 2001. "A Study of Smoothing Methods for Language Models Applied to Ad Hoc Information Retrieval." *Proceedings of the 24th*

annual international ACM SIGIR conference on Research and development in information retrieval - SIGIR '01: 334–42. http://portal.acm.org/citation.cfm?doid=383952.384019.

46. Zhao, Lin et al. 2008. "Sentence Extraction Based Single Document Summarization by Sentence Extraction Based Single Document Summarization." *Information Processing and Management* 2(3): 1–12. http://cci.drexel.edu/faculty/thu/research-papers/dawak-547.pdf.

47. Zhao, Lin, Lide Wu, and Xuanjing Huang. 2009. "Using Query Expansion in Graph-Based Approach for Query-Focused Multi-Document Summarization." *Information Processing and Management* 45(1): 35–41. http://dx.doi.org/10.1016/j.ipm.2008.07.001.

48. Zhou, Liang, CY Lin, and Eduard Hovy. 2005. "A BE-Based Multi-Document Summarizer with Query Interpretation." *Proceedings of Document Understanding Conferences.* http://www.isi.edu/div3/div3/pubs/papers/zhou2005be.pdf%5Cnhttp://citeseerx.ist.psu.edu/viewdoc/summary?doi=10.1.1.112.6809.

Druck:
Canon Deutschland Business Services GmbH
im Auftrag der KNV-Gruppe
Ferdinand-Jühlke-Str. 7
99095 Erfurt